Co

GW00703472

FRED KINSEY

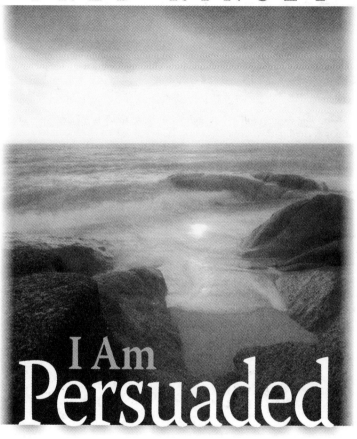

I Am
Persuaded

Pacific Press® Publishing Association
Nampa, Idaho
Oshawa, Ontario, Canada
www.pacificpress.com

Cover design by Gerald Lee Monks
Cover design resources from iStockphoto.com
Inside design by Aaron Troia

The author assumes full responsibility for the accuracy of all facts and quotations as cited in this book.

All Scripture quotations, unless otherwise noted, are from the King James Version.

Scriptures quoted from NASB are from *The New American Standard Bible*®, copyright © 1960, 1962, 1963, 1968, 1971, 1972, 1973, 1975, 1977, 1995 by The Lockman Foundation. Used by permission.

Scripture quotations marked NIV are from the HOLY BIBLE, NEW INTERNATIONAL VERSION®. Copyright © 1973, 1978, 1984 by International Bible Society. Used by permission of Zondervan Publishing House. All rights reserved.

Scriptures quoted from NKJV are from The New King James Version, copyright © 1979, 1980, 1982, Thomas Nelson, Inc., Publishers.

You can obtain additional copies of this book by calling toll-free 1-800-765-6955 or by visiting http://www.adventistbookcenter.com.

ISBN 13: 978-0-8163-2448-4 (pbk.)
ISBN 10: 0-8163-2448-4 (pbk.)

10 11 12 13 14 • 1 2 3 4 5

Introduction
A Letter of Love

Have you ever encountered a Bible passage that grabbed hold of your soul, held on, and wouldn't let you go until it had totally transformed your life?

I have.

And I want to share that text and the chapters that surround it, from one of the greatest love letters ever written—the New Testament book of Romans.

I'll tell you in a moment just which Bible verse seized me by the heartstrings and taught me to sing an entirely new song. But right now, by way of introduction, I want to share another verse—one found right at the heart of Romans. It's one that I quote often on *Voice of Prophecy* radio broadcasts. It's Romans 8:38, 39, which I usually recite from the good old King James Version. It goes like this: "For I am persuaded, that neither death, nor life, nor angels, nor principalities, nor powers, nor things present, nor things to come, nor height, nor depth, nor any other creature, shall be able to separate us from the love of God, which is in Christ Jesus our Lord."

This verse contains

- the assurance of God's love for me;
- the assurance that God's love extends to everyone who will receive it;
- the assurance that God's everlasting concern for planet Earth is founded on nothing less than the life and sacrificial death of Jesus Christ.

I Am Persuaded

It's that assurance that has become the bedrock of my faith—the bedrock of my life. It is the hope by which I live, and the message that I proclaim to the world.

But it's not the verse that originally transformed my life.

I'm going to keep you waiting for that.

First a little background.

I was raised by loving, Christian parents, but I was raised in an era and a community where religion—at least as I experienced it—tended to focus more on behavior than on faith.

Now, don't get me wrong. Religion ought to include aspects of behavior. A religion that doesn't change how you live is nothing more than a philosophy.

But it's easy for some people to get so focused on good behavior—even using religious motivations to try to change other people's behaviors—that faith and grace get lost in a huge pile of performance expectations. And the result is that religious people end up carrying around a tremendous sense of guilt and inadequacy—a sense that you can never keep all the rules precisely enough to please God.

Have you ever felt that way?

I did.

And for a time, I rebelled against that feeling of guilt by turning a deaf ear to religion. I didn't reject it totally. I just put it off to the side and tried not to think about all the things I was doing wrong—or at least not doing well enough.

But still, niggling away at the back of my mind, there was a tremendous sense of inadequacy. A sense that I could never be good enough, that the requirements of the gospel went far beyond what I could ever fulfill. And somewhere, hidden in the clutter of secular thoughts, there was still that feeling that I ought to be trying harder, ought to be doing better, or I was going to lose my soul.

A Letter of Love

Sound familiar?

If so, if you've ever felt that way, I have really, really good news for you. And it's found in the verse that transformed my life.

But there I was, as a young man, feeling condemned; feeling that I could never be religious enough to please God.

And then God started talking to me.

Not audibly. But I could hear His voice. I could hear His call.

And do you know what He was saying?

Fred . . . Fred . . . Fred . . . It was almost like when He called Samuel in the Old Testament. Now, I'm neither a prophet nor the son of a prophet. But I could hear the call of the Lord.

And He was calling me: the guilt-laden, weighed-down prodigal who thought he would be happier if he could completely tune out any spiritual influence in his life.

He found me in a rock music radio station, playing the top forty hits at top volume, and He told me in that still, small voice; He told me—the one who didn't want to hear His voice—that He wanted me to become a preacher and proclaim His message to others.

Frankly, I wanted to do anything but that. And I tried every way I knew to put off that call. But finally, there came a day when I told God, "All right. I'll go to the seminary, but here's the deal. If this works out OK, I'll be Your man. If not, You get off my back and leave me alone!"

That's the attitude I started the seminary with.

And in all honesty, I probably was hoping for option two—that God would quit bothering me, and I could get on with living life "My Way."

But then, in the second quarter of the seminary, I took an elective course on the book of Romans. In class I met Dr. Ivan

Blazen. *And* I met God in a whole new way.

It happened while we were studying chapter 3.

Today, looking back on that experience, I can see that my life can be divided into two eras: *Before Romans* and *After Romans*.

Before Romans I had a wonderful sense of Christian ethics, of right and wrong, of dos and don'ts. But I never experienced any of the joy, the peace, or the hope that a Christian ought to have.

Before Romans I knew I wasn't good enough to go to heaven. No matter how hard I tried, I always fell way short of what God wanted. The harder I tried, the harder I fell. And with each fall, it was harder to get up. Finally, I was tempted to *give* up, not *get up*.

Before Romans I might have looked good on the outside, but inside I knew I was lost.

Then, in the seminary, I read the book of Romans, and a flood of light poured into my life.

Today, I'm thankful to tell you, I'm living in the *After Romans* era. The book is still shining light into my life! Never does a day go by that I don't claim the promises, the hope, and the assurance that is so powerfully portrayed in Romans.

The great Reformer Martin Luther thought that everyone should memorize the entire book of Romans. But if you're not any better at memorization than I am, he had a suggestion for you as well. He said that, because there is so much wonderful light shining from its pages, we ought to at least read something from it every day.

Read something from Romans every day. Just think how that would brighten up your life!

And that's something I *can* do. How about you? Wouldn't you like to have such great light shining into your life every day—maybe when you first get up in the morning?

In this book I want to share the light that means so much to me. I will focus my attention on the first eight chapters of Romans, for that is where my soul found a deep revelation of the love that God has for me.

These chapters begin by illustrating the trouble that humanity is in apart from the salvation found in Jesus Christ.

For example, read Romans 3:10, "There is none righteous, no, not one."

No, not one, and that includes Mother Teresa and your kindly grandmother and the young heroes who give their lives for their countries. No exceptions.

But the good news is that Romans doesn't end on that hopeless note. It also offers the solution. It offers just exactly the hope that my guilt-worn heart needed.

The great theme of Romans is that, yes, I am not good enough and never will or can be good enough to be righteous before God. But Jesus Christ, who represents the righteousness of God Himself, is good enough, more than good enough. And by faith I stand covered in His righteousness and claim it as my own.

And now to the verse that seized me by the heartstrings and wouldn't let me go. It follows one of the most-quoted verses in the Bible. But I don't believe I had ever heard it mentioned in a sermon or in a Bible class in my entire life.

The verse I had heard—the one that preachers liked to wax eloquent on—was Romans 3:23, "For all have sinned and fall short of the glory of God" (NIV). I knew that verse by heart.

I knew that verse *in* my heart.

But somehow verse 24, the very next verse, had escaped me. It had never been brought to my attention.

Here's what it says, "And are justified freely by his grace through the redemption that came by Christ Jesus" (NIV).

My heart, weighed down with a load of guilt I could never

get rid of, almost leaped out of my chest when the weight of that verse landed on it. Because that verse is as light as a feather. It's as light as a feather but strong enough to lift all the other garbage that I was storing in my heart, and throw it clean away!

That day I discovered that I could have a clean heart. And my heart leaped for joy. I wanted to sing with the psalmist, "He has put a new song in my mouth—Praise to our God" (Psalm 40:3, NKJV)!

How did the redemption—this cleanness of heart—come? Did it come by our good works, by our acts of obedience, or by our faithfulness to God's commands? No, it came "by Christ Jesus." The King James Version reads, "Being justified freely by his grace through the redemption *that is in Christ Jesus*" (emphasis added).

Where is the redemption found? In me? In my good works? In your good works? In Paul's good works? No, the redemption is found *in Jesus*. Our redemption is in Him, and in what He did for us, in the perfect life that He lived and that He offers to each of us as a gift.

It's a *gift*! Do you get that? This featherweight relief for your heart's heavy burdens is a *gift*! Given freely by God through Jesus Christ our Savior.

Have you claimed this gift for yourself? Have you felt the burdens being lifted from your heart?

I hope so. And as you continue reading here about the book of Romans, I hope that this will be your daily experience. In the upcoming chapters we're going to explore the depths of the greatest love letter in the Bible, wrestle with some difficult passages, keep our eyes on Jesus, and learn from Him the secrets of eternal life in the kingdom of God.

The Power of God
Romans 1

It was a small story, buried in the *New York Times* on December 21, 1924, next to some ads for furs, Oriental rugs, and pianos. The tiny headline read, "Hitler Tamed by Prison."

> Adolph Hitler, once the demi-god of reactionary extremists, was released on parole from imprisonment at Fortress Landsburg, Bavaria, today and immediately left in an auto for Munich. He looked a much sadder and wiser man today than last spring when he, with Ludendorff and other radical extremists, appeared before a Munich court charged with conspiracy to overthrow the Government.
>
> His behavior during imprisonment convinced the authorities that, like his political organization . . . [he] was no longer to be feared. It is believed he will retire to private life and return to Austria, the country of his birth.[1]

To be fair, who in 1924 would have ever thought that within nine years a supposedly tamed demagogue would become the Führer, and lead the people into the most destructive war the world had ever seen?

Such a thought would have been inconceivable at that time. It was, after all, just six years since the end of what was then known as the Great War, or "the war to end all wars."

According to the best minds of the time, the twentieth century should have been characterized by peace, harmony, and advancement, not by the two greatest human conflagrations of history.

I Am Persuaded

At the beginning of the twentieth century, the optimism and enthusiasm were so strong they could be felt in the air. People believed that humanity was on an incredible path of moral, social, and scientific progress. The ignorances, the superstitions, and the barbarism of previous centuries were going to be relics of a decrepit past and would have no place in the enlightened future.

Consider the following, taken from a speech given just a decade or so before the twentieth century opened.

> Therefore, gentlemen, we will not be shaken in our belief that our research and inventive activity leads mankind to higher levels of culture, ennobling it and making it more accessible to ideal aspirations, that the impending scientific age will diminish its hardships and its sickness, enhance its enjoyment of life, and make it better, happier, and more content with its fate.[2]

Wonderful, optimistic sentiments.

They were spoken by Werner von Siemens, founder of the well-known Siemens company, in a speech given in—of all places—Berlin, Germany.

How ironic that much of the destruction and violence of the twentieth century's wars came about directly as a result of the advances made in the "impending scientific age" that Herr Siemens thought would usher in a moral and technological utopia.

But the irony leads to my point. Many centuries earlier, the apostle Paul, writing a letter to the church in Rome, gave a description of humanity and human nature that presaged just how futile and misguided all this optimism really was.

If there's one thing that Paul makes clear at the beginning of his letter to the Romans, it is that humanity is sinful and in need of redemption.

But I don't think we need Paul to teach us that humanity is evil. Just pick up the daily paper or read the headlines on the Yahoo! Web site.

No, we need the apostle Paul to show us just how futile and misguided all attempts at moral progress and salvation are *apart from the gospel of Jesus Christ.*

That's why in Romans 1 (after a long introduction in which Paul speaks directly to the believers in Rome, expressing his desire to visit them) the apostle shares a central truth not only of the book of Romans but of the Bible itself, a truth about human depravity *and* the solution to that depravity—the gospel.

Paul writes,

> For I am not ashamed of the gospel, for it is the power of God for salvation to everyone who believes, to the Jew first and also to the Greek. For in it the righteousness of God is revealed from faith to faith; as it is written, "BUT THE RIGHTEOUS man SHALL LIVE BY FAITH."
>
> For the wrath of God is revealed from heaven against all ungodliness and unrighteousness of men who suppress the truth in unrighteousness, because that which is known about God is evident within them; for God made it evident to them (Romans 1:16–19, NASB).

Notice here the first thing that Paul says about the gospel. It is the "power of *God* for salvation" (emphasis added). It's not the power of human reason and intellect that brings salvation. Nor is it the power of human science, as Siemens had hoped. No, it is the "power of God."

Think about what this means. The visible universe, the

universe that we can see, is billions of light-years across in diameter. And yet scientists speculate that this visible universe comprises only a small portion of what is really out there. The rest we can't see.

Now when Paul talks about the power of God, he's talking about the same incredible power that created the universe, the part we can and can't see. That's a lot of power! And the good news is that *this* is the same incredible power that is at work for our salvation.

In other words, salvation is something that God, using His incredible power, does *for us* because we can't do it for ourselves. *If the power that created the universe is working to save us, how could we be lost, other than by our own choice?*

Paul then touches on a core thought in his letter to the Romans. He says that in the gospel *"the righteousness of God"* is revealed (emphasis added). He just finished talking about "the power of God," and now he is talking about the "righteousness of God."

Again, it's all God. The gospel is the power of God for salvation, and that salvation comes through the "righteousness of God," which is revealed in the gospel. And that's because the message of the gospel is salvation for humans *only* through the righteousness of God, which is credited to us—given to us—by faith.

And this leads into the great theme of Romans, the theme that has literally changed the course of history. Now quoting the Old Testament, Paul writes, "BUT THE RIGHTEOUS man SHALL LIVE BY FAITH."

It is by faith that we take hold of the "righteousness of God" as revealed in the gospel. We are sinners, we have violated God's law, and we have no righteousness and goodness in and of ourselves; therefore we are condemned to face the "wrath of God."

In fact, that is what Paul says in the next verse: "For *the wrath of God* is revealed from heaven against all ungodliness and unrighteousness of men who suppress the truth in unrighteousness" (verse 18; emphasis added).

Notice, we have seen the "power of God," the "righteousness of God," and now the "wrath of God"—all in these few verses. The gospel is the "power of God," in which the "righteousness of God" is revealed by how He saves from the "wrath of God" all who live by faith in Jesus.

Paul then spends the rest of the chapter depicting the sorry state of humanity and why it deserves God's wrath. This reality forms the background for the wonderful news that none of us, no matter how deserving of it, needs to face this wrath because Jesus faced it for us at the cross.

Or as the author Ellen White so beautifully put it:

> Christ was treated as we deserve, that we might be treated as He deserves. He was condemned for our sins, in which He had no share, that we might be justified by His righteousness, in which we had no share. He suffered the death which was ours, that we might receive the life which was His.[3]

This is the foundation that Paul is setting down in the first chapter of Romans. Read from verse 18 to the end of the chapter. Paul paints a pretty solemn picture of humanity; there's no optimism about human progress.

Unfortunately, human history has proven his bleak assessment to be correct.

And yet the whole point, beginning with this chapter, is to show that no matter how bad the situation, God has a solution. And that solution is the gospel—"the power of God for salvation to everyone who believes, to the Jew first and also to the Greek."

His phrase "to the Jew first and also to the Greek" is just another way of referring to all of humanity. His point is that anyone who believes—regardless of ethnic or national background—who comes to Jesus in faith, trusting in His righteousness, which is the "righteousness of God," can have salvation.

The solution to the problem is big enough to embrace everyone who claims it by faith. And that's because the solution is found in Jesus and what He has done for us; it's never in ourselves and never can be.

Jesus died for us, so we can have eternal life. He died for you and for me. No matter what our lives have been, we can claim His perfect life in our place.

A man who was about to be executed for a horrible crime, admitted, "I've lived a rough life." But then he went on to ask a question I think we all should ask, "I wonder if God has a place for people like me."

I have to confess.

I've wondered the same thing about myself.

It's not that I've done anything I could be executed for.

But still, I know my life isn't worthy of being extended for eternity!

Is there a place in God's eternal kingdom for a person like me?

Yes!

But only because of Jesus.

Only because of the gospel, the "power of God for salvation" for people like me.

My only claim to that salvation is my desperate need.

Your only claim to salvation is your utter need.

But the message of Romans is *that is enough*!

That is enough because, as Paul affirms at the heart of this great book,

> neither death, nor life, nor angels, nor principalities, nor powers, nor things present, nor things to come, nor height, nor depth, nor any other creature, shall be able to separate us from the love of God, which is in Christ Jesus our Lord (Romans 8:38, 39, KJV).

God's grace is enough to save us from our sins, and it's also enough to do something more in our lives, to do something to our hearts. We'll look at just what that is in the next chapter.

---

1. "Hitler Tamed by Prison," *New York Times,* December 21, 1924.

2. A. Hermann, "Auf eine höhere Stufe des Daseins erheben," 812, quoted in Rüdiger Safranski, *Martin Heidegger: Between Good and Evil,* trans. Ewald Osers (Cambridge, Mass.: Harvard University Press, 1998), 35.

3. Ellen G. White, *The Desire of Ages* (Mountain View, Calif.: Pacific Press® Publishing Association, 1940), 25.

"The Goodness of God"
Romans 2

I've been a minister of the gospel for many years now, and I have preached all sorts of sermons. And though I can look back at some and shake my head, wondering, *What was I thinking when I said that?* I can honestly say that I have never preached a homily like the one given recently in York, England; a sermon in which the pastor told his people to go out and shoplift.

You might find it hard to believe that a pastor would preach a sermon telling his people to go out and shoplift. So I'm going to directly quote here, from a transcript of the sermon, the words of the preacher. I quote,

> My advice, as a Christian priest, is to shoplift.
>
> I do not offer such advice because I think that stealing is a good thing, or because I think that it is harmless, for it is neither. I would ask that they [the poor, former prisoners] steal not from small family businesses but from large national businesses, knowing that the costs are ultimately passed on to the rest of us in the form of higher prices. I would ask them not to take any more than they need, for any longer than they need. . . .
>
> What, then, of the . . . [c]ommandment, "Thou shalt not steal"? Is this advice to usurp the authority of Almighty God?
>
> No.[1]

I'm glad the priest in question didn't think he was usurping or countermanding God's commandments. But I'm not sure I follow his logic.

When you tell people to steal, aren't you going against God, who said, "Thou shalt not steal" (Exodus 20:15)?

Still, I'm not passing judgment on the minister. Why?

Because my topic here is the second chapter of the book of Romans, where the apostle Paul cautions,

> Therefore you have no excuse, everyone of you who passes judgment, for in that which you judge another, you condemn yourself; for you who judge practice the same things. And we know that the judgment of God rightly falls upon those who practice such things (Romans 2:1, 2, NASB).

So I am not here to pass judgment on this minister because by so doing I would condemn myself. Sure, I haven't preached exactly that kind of sermon. But I've been guilty of things just as bad, of things that God could rightly judge and condemn. God might even see them as being worse than what that preacher did.

Turning to Romans 2, notice that Paul continues what he started in Romans 1, which is to point out the sorry state of humanity.

This concept was central to his theology. Only now, instead of talking about humanity in general as he did in the previous chapter, he's getting a little more specific, talking to the Jews in particular, or even to the church itself, which at that time was still composed mostly of Jews. And what he is saying is that basically *you are sinners just as the pagans are, so don't be so quick to condemn in others what you are guilty of yourself, and that is— sin.*

We're all sinners. We're all guilty. I've been told that even the late comedian George Carlin, who wasn't known as a particularly clean-mouthed commentator, was heard to say,

> I'm tired of hearing about innocent victims. It's fiction. If you live on this planet you're guilty, period, . . . next case, end of report. Your birth certificate is proof of guilt.[2]

Well, it may be just a comedian's commentary, but it catches a major theme of Romans, especially Romans 2. Here Paul writes about the judgment of God that is going to fall on everyone who doesn't live the kind of life that reveals true saving faith in Jesus.

In Romans 1, Paul laid out how the pagans had fallen into idolatry and sin, and would be judged accordingly. Now, though, he comes to those who profess to know the true God, those who have His law—those who think that they might have something in and of themselves, either by virtue of their birth or by virtue of their law-keeping, which can give them merit before God.

And, as we'll see, Paul will have none of that. Instead, he overtly and without pulling any punches shows just how guilty we *all* are before God. Listen to what he writes.

> But if you bear the name "Jew" and rely upon the Law and boast in God, and know His will and approve the things that are essential, being instructed out of the Law, and are confident that you yourself are a guide to the blind, a light to those who are in darkness, a corrector of the foolish, a teacher of the immature, having in the Law the embodiment of knowledge and of the truth, you, therefore, who teach another, do you not teach yourself?

You who preach that one shall not steal, do you steal? You who say that one should not commit adultery, do you commit adultery? You who abhor idols, do you rob temples? You who boast in the Law, through your breaking the Law, do you dishonor God? For "THE NAME OF GOD IS BLASPHEMED AMONG THE GENTILES BECAUSE OF YOU," just as it is written (Romans 2:17–24, NASB).

For Paul, the solution to this guilt isn't found in any outward acts of piety or rules or laws. Though Paul, as we will see in later chapters of Romans, is not opposed to the law or obedience to the law, he wants everyone to understand that salvation isn't found in the law or in anything other than faith in Jesus and in His righteousness, a faith that expresses itself in a new life here and now.

That's why Paul in Romans 2 talks about circumcision, but in a strange way. He says that true circumcision is "of the heart" (verse 29, NASB). God wants us to be changed inwardly through the working of His spirit on hearts that are surrendered in love to Him. Outward forms and rules and regulations, in and of themselves, are useless for salvation. They can't bring life any more than stuffing food in the mouth of a corpse could bring life to the corpse.

No, instead, we look to the Cross, we see the Cross, and we see the goodness of God revealed in the most remarkable way imaginable—He, the Lord, bearing in Himself the punishment for our sins. We see the Son of God crucified, not because He deserved it but because we did and He wants to spare us from the punishment that our acts and deeds deserve. And the only way He can do that, the only way He can be "just, and the justifier of him which believeth in Jesus" (Romans 3:26, KJV) is through dying in our stead at Calvary.

No wonder Paul writes in Romans 2, "Or despisest thou the

riches of his goodness and forbearance and longsuffering; not knowing that the goodness of God leadeth thee to repentance?" (verse 4, KJV).

Every one of us—no matter who we are—are beneficiaries in one way or another of God's "goodness and forbearance and longsuffering." Our mere existence, the miracle of life itself, our ability to think and to love—these are all gifts from God. But the greatest revelation, the greatest gift, the greatest expression of God's goodness is the Cross.

If that doesn't lead you to repentance, what would? If that doesn't lead you to want to surrender your sinful ways to God and be given a new heart, a circumcised heart, and thus a new life in Christ, what would?

I've heard people ask the question "Is the universe friendly?" Well, on the face of it, it might not seem that way. Here we are, stranded on the third rock from the sun in a vast, cold cosmos that seems entirely indifferent to us or to our existence. It makes me think of the poem by Stephen Crane called "A Man Said to the Universe."

> A man said to the universe:
> "Sir I exist!"
> "However," replied the universe,
> "The fact has not created in me
> A sense of obligation."[3]

That's a sentiment that you could easily come to, were it not for one thing, and that is the Cross. So I would like to revise that poem like this:

> A man said to the universe:
> "Sir I exist!"

"The Goodness of God"

And the Lord who created the universe replied,

"I know that you do, and I love you, and I want to give you a new life now and the hope and promise of eternal life in a world made new, and you can have all that through Jesus, who died for your sins."

"Is the universe friendly?" Yes, because the God who created it also gave Himself for us and by so doing, linked Himself to us and to our humanity with ties that can never be broken.

You are a sinner. I am a sinner. Jew, Gentile, we are all sinners. Even a foul-mouthed comedian knows this; "Your birth certificate is proof of guilt," he said.

But that's not the end of the story.

Thank God, that's not the end of the story.

The word *Guilty* can be erased from your birth certificate!

No, that's not right.

It can't be erased.

But it can be marked out—marked out in red—in the blood of Jesus Christ, shed for the express purpose of covering your sins and mine, shed for covering that word *Guilty* on your birth certificate and putting His perfect, guiltless life in its place.

That's what the gospel is all about. That's what the book of Romans is all about. That's why Paul can say, right in the heart of this letter to the Romans:

> I am persuaded, that neither death, nor life, nor angels, nor principalities, nor powers, nor things present, nor things to come, nor height, nor depth, nor any other creature, shall be able to separate us from the love of God, which is in Christ Jesus our Lord (Romans 8:38, 39, KJV).

But how does this change lives? How does it really make a difference in the way I live day by day? That's the topic I want to take up in chapter 3.

---

1. Tim Jones, "A Sermon for the Fourth Sunday of Advent" (sermon, Church of St. Lawrence, York, England, December 20, 2009), quoted in "Desperation Theology," *Harper's Magazine,* March 2010, 18.

2. George Carlin, *Napalm & Silly Putty* (New York: Hyperion, 2001), 46.

3. Stephen Crane, "A Man Said to the Universe," in *War Is Kind* (New York: University Press, 1899).

"Being Justified Freely by His Grace"
Romans 3

If there is one theme in Romans that comes through clearly, especially in the opening chapters, it is the utter depravity of humanity. Paul wrote these words almost two thousand years ago, but the events of the past hundred years are more than enough to prove his point. The past twenty would do the trick, don't you think?

No wonder, then, the apostle Paul—after showing that both Jews and Gentiles are guilty before God—could sum up in Romans 3 all that he had written so far with these powerful words, which he is quoting from Psalms:

> As it is written, There is none righteous, no, not one: There is none that understandeth, there is none that seeketh after God. They are all gone out of the way, they are together become unprofitable; there is none that doeth good, no, not one. Their throat is an open sepulchre; with their tongues they have used deceit; the poison of asps is under their lips: Whose mouth is full of cursing and bitterness: Their feet are swift to shed blood: Destruction and misery are in their ways: And the way of peace have they not known: There is no fear of God before their eyes (Romans 3:10–18).

Yes, for the first few chapters of Romans, Paul explicitly shows the very sad and sorry state of humanity. And who could argue with him?

But now we come to the greatest part of Romans, the part

that has changed countless lives, mine included. You see, I come from a family of preachers—got them on both sides. As I mentioned in the introduction, as a young man, I found myself rather reluctantly at the seminary. There I told God that I would study, that I would seek to know Him, and that if it worked, great; if not, then would He just, please, get off my back?

When I opened the book of Romans there at the seminary, I hate to admit it, but I don't think that I had ever even read it before. As I read the initial chapters, the ones that so painfully but accurately depict human depravity, I found it easy to relate to Paul's message, especially Romans 3:23, "For all have sinned, and come short of the glory of God." That was a truth I didn't need Inspiration to tell me. It was a painful fact of my daily existence.

But then, in an electrifying moment, in a moment that has changed my life, I came to the very next verse: "For all have sinned, and come short of the glory of God; *being justified freely by his grace through the redemption that is in Christ Jesus*" (verse 24; emphasis added).

"Being justified freely by his grace through the redemption that is in Christ Jesus"?

In other words, Paul spent all this time talking about the problem, talking about the desperate situation we humans are in, and then, in just a few words, he offered the solution. *"Justified freely by his grace through the redemption that is in Christ Jesus"* (emphasis added).

Here is the beacon that my life is focused on. We have fallen, and we will fall far short of God's glory. But we have no fear of the future because salvation comes to us through grace, through the merit credited to us by faith *without the deeds of the law*.

As a law keeper, as someone who believes in the validity of God's law, I can't tell you how liberating, how freeing, how wonderful it was to realize that my salvation rested, not in my keeping of the law, but in the righteousness of Jesus, whose perfect law-keeping becomes credited to me, as if it were mine.

And it comes to me and you *by faith alone.*

Here is the heart and soul of the gospel, of the plan of salvation, *of the entire message of the Bible.* From the fall of Adam and Eve in Eden, right up through the last pages in the book of Revelation, the message of God to our sinful, fallen world is that you can be accepted by God, no matter how wretched your condition, because of what Jesus has done for you.

The liar, the cheater, the adulterer, the murderer—it doesn't matter. What matters is that through the grace of Christ, who died for your sins, you can stand pardoned, forgiven, and justified, not because of what you have done but *despite it.*

That's the whole point! What we have done is, indeed, precisely what has condemned us. The good news is that salvation comes from faith in what Jesus has done *for us,* because what we have done is, well, what we have already read. Paul described it in graphic terms. That's why we have to be saved by something other than our works, and the good news is that we are. We are saved by the deeds of Jesus, which Paul in Romans 3 calls "the righteousness of God" (verse 21). And if "the righteousness of God" can't save us, what can?

Listen to these other words from Romans 3.

> Therefore by the deeds of the law there shall no flesh be justified in his sight: for by the law is the knowledge of sin. But now the righteousness of God without the law is manifested, being witnessed by the law and the prophets; Even the righteousness of God which is by faith of Jesus Christ unto all and upon all them that believe: for there is no difference (verses 20–22).

Or these, "Therefore we conclude that a man is justified by faith without the deeds of the law" (verse 28).

"Even the righteousness of God which is by faith of Jesus Christ unto all and upon all them that believe." What is he saying? He is saying that though we are sinners, though we have violated God's law, the very "righteousness of God" Himself becomes ours, becomes credited to us by faith in Jesus. Here's why Paul stresses that a "man is justified by faith *without the deeds of the law*" (emphasis added). And that's because the law, however important, cannot save you. Instead, the law shows why you *nee*d to be saved. The law is like a mirror. It shows me my wrinkles, but staring at my reflected wrinkles all day isn't going to get rid of them!

Let me repeat the two verses that capture the essence of the Creator God's message to each of us, Romans 3:23, 24, "For all have sinned, and come short of the glory of God; being justified freely by his grace through the redemption that is in Christ Jesus."

The problem is easy to see. Sin is all around us. Or, even more painful, it's in us. When was the last time you took a close look deep inside your own heart?

You don't need some zombie movie or slasher flick to find a scary place. Your own heart will do.

That's the problem. But then, right after the problem, the solution comes—we are justified, forgiven, and pardoned *freely* by His grace through Jesus Christ the Lord.

Freely! That's the whole point of grace. You're given something that you don't deserve and can't earn. Don't wait until you feel deserving of it. You don't deserve it, never can, and never will. That's what makes the promise so wonderful.

I can't tell you how much this truth has changed my life, and still continues to change it, because it is a truth that I, Pastor

"Being Justified Freely by His Grace"

Fred Kinsey, a sinner, have to cling to every day. It's a truth that changed the life of Martin Luther and, through his work, has changed the world.

And it is a truth that can change your life.

You know, I don't get into politics at the Voice of Prophecy. I'm interested in only one Ruler, the Lord Jesus Christ. But a while back, someone asked a politician turned TV host about his Christian faith. Because he's known as a Christian, he said that he believed there was only one way to heaven, which is through faith in Jesus Christ, because that's what the New Testament says.

But then he diluted his testimony with what seemed like political backpedaling to me. Referring to the New Testament, he said, "That's the only map I got. Someone says, Well, I got a different map. OK! If it works, I am not going to argue with you."

That might be good politics, but it's bad theology. If your map doesn't point you to the righteousness of Jesus credited to you by faith without the deeds of the law, if your map doesn't point you to the promise that any one of us, no matter what our pasts are, can have salvation in Jesus, not because we are worthy but because He is worthy, and God's grace credits His worthiness to us by faith—then that map is leading you in the wrong direction.

Because the fact is that Paul is right. We are all sinners. Maybe you haven't killed anyone or robbed a bank. But that doesn't mean you've lived a perfect life. I'm not a criminal by the world's standards. But I am a sinner by God's standards. I'm not worthy of eternal life.

But that doesn't negate the good news found in the book of Romans—the great good news that even sinners like you and I can be "justified freely by [God's] grace through the redemption that is in Christ Jesus."

I Am Persuaded

That's why I so cherish the words of Romans 8:38, 39.

For I am persuaded, that neither death, nor life, nor angels, nor principalities, nor powers, nor things present, nor things to come, nor height, nor depth, nor any other creature, shall be able to separate us from the love of God, which is in Christ Jesus our Lord.

But who all does that "us" include? Are there people who God automatically loves because they're nice people and others that He can't quite work up a positive reaction to? Stay with me for chapter 4, where we'll look at just how far God's love extends.

"The Troubling Gospel"
Romans 4

July 29, 1976. 1:10 A.M. A warm night in the Bronx.

Eighteen-year-old Donna Lauria started to get out of a car parked in front of her parents' apartment. She and her girlfriend Jody had been sitting there visiting for a few minutes. When she opened the car door to go into the apartment, a man rushed up to her. Startled, Donna said, "What is this?"

Those were her last words.

The man pulled a handgun, crouched, and fired three shots. The first killed Donna, the second wounded Jody, and the third missed both women.

Thus began the reign of terror that came to be known as the Son of Sam killings. For a year, people all over New York City found themselves looking over their shoulders, wondering if perfect strangers might suddenly pull a gun and open fire.

By the time police finally arrested David Berkowitz the next summer, the young man was willing to confess to killing six people and wounding seven others. Pleading guilty at his trial, he received six consecutive life sentences.

Fast-forward thirty years to 2006, the year David Berkowitz's book *Son of Hope* hit bookstores. You might be surprised to learn that in the intervening years, David has become a born-again Christian. His book, *Son of Hope,* tells of his past life and then of his experience with Christ in prison.

And while I was glad to hear that David has given his heart to the Lord, I must admit to feeling a sense of relief when I learned that he won't receive any royalties for his writing efforts. Instead, a portion of the proceeds will go to his victims and their families.

I Am Persuaded

David has many supporters who see in his story an example of the amazing grace of God, who forgives and who changes lives. David says, " 'These friendships, relationships, are a precious and priceless gift from God. . . . Here I am, a convicted felon, a murderer, a man undeserving of anything that is good and wholesome. Yet, there are people who have found it in their heart to love me and have concern for me.' "[1]

What can I say other than that's what the gospel is about: you getting from God what you do not deserve—forgiveness, salvation, and the promise of eternal life. And that promise reaches even to the Son of Sam.

David Berkowitz, though, was a Boy Scout compared to some other criminals. Remember Jeffrey Dahmer? He killed many more people than Berkowitz. And he was sentenced to life in prison *with no parole.*

Did you know that Dahmer also claimed Christ as his Savior and was baptized? He was murdered by another prisoner shortly after that.

Now think with me for a moment. Notorious serial killer Jeffrey Dahmer died a believer in Jesus, claiming the righteousness of Christ as his own. Does that mean he died *with the promise of eternal life?*

Does that question trouble you?

In the first three chapters of Romans, we saw very clearly that Paul's point is that all humanity, Jew and Gentile, are sinners. We have all fallen short of the glory of God, but we can have the forgiveness of sins "through the redemption that is in Christ Jesus" (Romans 3:24).

There's no mention here of some people's sins being worse than others. We all are sinners, and none of us is going to be redeemed by anything but the grace of God. No matter how major or minor our sins.

Yes, it's grace and that means it's undeserved, a theme that Paul expounds upon in Romans 4.

Now, what's fascinating here is the example that Paul uses. He doesn't talk about serial killers needing grace. Instead, he retells the story of one of the Old Testament giants of faith, one of the most revered holy men of old, the patriarch of patriarchs, as an example of someone who needed to be saved, not by the works of the law but by God's grace alone.

Here is what Paul tells us about Abraham in Romans 4:1–3:

> What then shall we say that Abraham, our forefather according to the flesh, has found? For if Abraham was justified by works, he has something to boast about, but not before God. For what does the Scripture say? "ABRAHAM BELIEVED GOD, AND IT WAS CREDITED TO HIM AS RIGHTEOUSNESS" (NASB).

Paul is quoting from the first book of the Bible, Genesis, to teach the great theme that permeates all of Scripture—salvation by faith in Jesus. The text is Genesis 15:6, which says that Abraham "believed in the LORD; and He reckoned it to him as righteousness" (NASB).

It was reckoned to him as righteousness. The theological term is *imputed,* which means it was granted to him, even though he wasn't actually righteous. He was just *considered* righteous by God.

He didn't earn it. He *couldn't* earn it. That is Paul's point. If he could earn it, it wouldn't be grace; it would be a debt *owed him.* And Paul wants to dissuade us from thinking that if we just work hard enough at it we can earn salvation. In the next verse, Paul writes, "Now to him that worketh is the reward not reckoned of grace, but of debt" (Romans 4:4, KJV).

A debt? That would mean that it was *owed* to him. And if the Bible teaches anything, it teaches that none of us are *owed* salvation and that none of us are or could ever be good enough to be owed it—not in the same way that someone owes you for the work that you do for him or her.

This is precisely why Paul says that even for a giant of faith such as Abraham—a man with many good works—salvation still had to be by grace, a gift from God apart from the works of the law.

Paul continues later in the chapter, stressing that Abraham was counted righteous before God even before he was circumcised, meaning that he was an example of salvation by faith both for the Gentile and the Jew. This is important because he stresses in the earlier chapters that as far as salvation goes, Jew or Gentile, it makes no difference: we are all sinners in need of God's grace, and this cannot come from obedience to God's law, no matter how important obedience is.

So Paul writes,

> It was not through law that Abraham and his off-spring received the promise that he would be heir of the world, but through the righteousness that comes by faith. For if those who live by law are heirs, faith has no value and the promise is worthless, because law brings wrath. And where there is no law there is no transgression (verses 13–15, NIV).

Don't miss this important point, please! Even in the immediate context of Abraham's physical heirs, the Jews, whom God specifically told to obey the law, righteousness came by faith not by works of the law. He says that the promise of eternal life is "worthless"—*worthless* if it comes through the law. The Greek word for *worthless* means "powerless, a waste, nullified." And that's because we are sinners, and as such, our works cannot cut it, cannot even come close to cutting it.

On the contrary, he says the law does what? The "law brings wrath," because the law is what points out sin. "Where there is no law," he wrote, "there is no transgression"—that is, there is no sin! Is he saying that there is no sin in this world? No! He's already put that idea to rest many times in the preceding chapters.

Paul isn't claiming that the law isn't to be kept. He never claims that, not here or anywhere. Instead, his point is that salvation is by grace not by keeping the law.

That's why he ends the chapter with the following:

The words "it was credited to him" [talking about what Genesis said regarding Abraham] were written not for him alone, but also for us, to whom God will *credit righteousness*—for us who believe in him who raised Jesus our Lord from the dead. He was delivered over to death for our sins and was raised to life for our justification (verses 23–25, NIV; emphasis added).

"To whom God will credit righteousness." What a wonderful promise! To have righteousness, God's righteousness, *credited* to us by faith—that, my friend, is the wonderful hope and promise of the Bible and that is Paul's message to us in Romans.

Yet it can be troubling, can't it? That means some pretty rough people can have salvation in Jesus, doesn't it?

I don't know David Berkowitz's heart; I just know the promises of God for salvation to all who accept Jesus as their Savior. I don't know the heart of Jeffrey Dahmer; I just know what the Bible says about grace even for the worst of sinners.

I Am Persuaded

It's troubling, I know, to think of serial killers in heaven. But Jesus Christ died even for people like them. He paid for their sins as well as mine. It is their privilege, as much as mine, to accept the perfect life of Jesus, the pure blood of Jesus, to cover the records of shameful lives.

No matter how bad a man's or woman's sins—no matter how bad my sins or your sins—you and I and Jeffrey Dahmer and David Berkowitz can all meet in heaven. We can all kneel at the feet of the Lamb of God "who takes away the sin of the world" (John 1:29, NIV), who bore our sins, all of our sins, on His wounded back.

On His broken heart.

In His shed blood.

The Savior who did that, who died on the cross, loves people.

He loves good people.

He loves bad people.

He loves even the worst of people.

And He loves you and me.

Every person who has the privilege of kneeling before his or her Savior in heaven will be there for one reason and one reason only: the righteousness of Christ credited to his or her account by the grace of God, and received by faith.

Each and every one of us can—must—cling to the precious words found at the heart of Paul's letter to the Romans:

> I am persuaded, that neither death, nor life, nor angels, nor principalities, nor powers, nor things present, nor things to come, nor height, nor depth, nor any other creature, shall be able to separate us from the love of God, which is in Christ Jesus our Lord (Romans 8:38, 39, KJV).

But the question remains, Is it possible to go too far? Is it possible to presume too much on the love and grace of God, and to miss out on salvation because of it? The answer we discover in chapter 5 may surprise you.

---

1. Serge F. Kovaleski, "Backers Give 'Son of Sam' Image Makeover," *New York Times,* July 13, 2010, New York edition, A18.

Grace Abounded Much More
Romans 5

One of the most dramatic and consequential events in modern history was the Bolshevik Revolution in Russia in 1917. Who had any idea that this revolution, which ended the three-hundred-year Romanov dynasty, would have such incredible consequences—not only for Russia, but for the world? By the time the Soviet Union finally collapsed in 1991, millions had been murdered, millions had been sent to prison, and millions had been forced to live under repressive regimes that stifled the most basic freedoms.

Consequences, indeed.

Though many forces were at work to undermine the reign of Tsar Nicholas II, historians generally agree that one of the factors that helped bring the regime down was the influence of a degenerate monk named Rasputin, who ingratiated himself with the tsar and his wife, Alexandra.

According to the story, the tsar's son, Alexei, suffered from hemophilia, a common disease among royalty. Supposedly, Rasputin, a self-styled faith healer, was able to bring the child some relief. Thus, he became a favorite in the Romanov court.

Rasputin, however, wasn't nicknamed the Mad Monk for nothing. Indeed, he was a degenerate drunk and a sexual pervert whose nefarious activities caused scandal after scandal, which strengthened the resolve of those striving to overthrow the tsar.

How, though, did this supposedly Christian monk justify his sinful behavior? He did so through the misapplication of one of the most famous texts in the Bible—a text that we are going to look at as we continue our study of the book of Romans.

Before we get to that text and to its misapplication, let's review what Romans' actual message is. (Actually, it's the message of the whole Bible.) It is the great truth of salvation by faith in Jesus Christ alone. What it all means can be boiled down to this: *no matter who you are, no matter your past, you can find forgiveness with God through the righteousness of Jesus.* This forgiveness is not anything that you can earn through your works. It comes to you by God's grace, and grace means you're given something that you do *not* deserve.

No, you do not deserve it, but you are given it anyway. It is a gift from a loving, caring God to a sinful, erring human. As we saw, too, some pretty nasty people have claimed that gift for themselves—even some of the worst criminals in history. And we also saw that some pretty holy people, such as Abraham, needed to claim that gift as well.

And that's because, according to the Bible, from the nicest to the nastiest among us, we are all sinners who need grace in order to be made right with God. The verses that, I think, say everything we need to know, are Romans 3:23, 24: "For all have sinned and fall short of the glory of God, being justified as a gift by His grace through the redemption which is in Christ Jesus" (NASB).

It's like this—we are sinners, we have done wrong, but we can be made right with God through the righteousness of Jesus, which is credited to us by faith and faith alone. It's what theologians call *justification by faith.*

In fact, the chapter that we are going to look at now, Romans 5, starts with this famous verse: "Therefore, having been *justified by faith,* we have peace with God through our Lord Jesus Christ" (Romans 5:1, NKJV; emphasis added). Notice because we are "justified by faith"—that is, because we are covered in the righteousness of Christ—we have what? Yes, "peace with God."

And that's because we know that this justification, this being made right with God, comes not by our works but by faith. We claim for ourselves what Jesus has done for us. We believe it by faith, and it becomes real in our lives. We don't have to be constantly worrying if we have done enough good works. In fact, it isn't possible to do enough good works. You *never can* have enough works.

The peace comes from knowing *that you don't have to.* Your salvation is in what Jesus has done for you; you rest assured in *His righteousness,* not your own. And this is what brings us the peace that Paul is talking about here.

This truth is what changed the life of Martin Luther. It has changed mine too. And God alone knows how many other lives have been transformed by this truth.

Indeed, this truth keeps getting better in Romans 5. Listen to what Paul writes a few verses later: "For when we were still without strength, in due time Christ died for the ungodly. For scarcely for a righteous man will one die; yet perhaps for a good man someone would even dare to die. But God demonstrates His own love toward us, in that while we were still sinners, Christ died for us" (verses 6–8, NKJV).

Think of what this means. "But God demonstrates His own love toward us, in that while we were still sinners, Christ died for us."

God loves us even as sinners, even when we are separated from Him, living in sin, living in ignorance of His grace and love. The point—and this fits right in with justification by faith—is that you don't have to do anything to earn God's love. The love is there, *already.* We don't generate that love; no, our only work is to *respond* to it, and that response is to claim for ourselves what Jesus has done for us. That response is to live by faith. Or as Paul reminded us earlier: "The just shall live by faith" (Romans 1:17, NKJV).

For a good portion of Romans 5, Paul talks about how Adam's

fall brought death and ruin upon humanity. His fall separated humanity from God, and that separation has caused the havoc and suffering that we see everywhere. Worse, it has brought death. The good news, however, is that Christ came to undo what Adam did. Through His life and death, Jesus reconciled humanity to God.

How does this work? Well, because of Adam, the whole world stood condemned before God. But, because of Christ, the whole world now stands *reconciled* to God. What this means is that instead of automatic condemnation because of what Adam did, anyone can be saved because of what Jesus did. All we have to do is surrender ourselves in faith to Christ. We then have the promise of eternal life. That is the reconciliation that Jesus wrought for us with the Father.

That's what grace is all about. We don't earn it, we don't deserve it, and there's nothing we can do either to earn or deserve it. Instead, it is given to us as a gift, a gift of God's grace. That's why it's called the "good news." Indeed, it's hard to imagine any news better than that.

Look at how Paul ends the chapter.

But where sin abounded, grace abounded much more, so that as sin reigned in death, even so grace might reign through righteousness to eternal life through Jesus Christ our Lord (Romans 5:20, 21, NKJV).

That's a powerful thought, isn't it? *Where sin abounded, God's grace abounded much more.* That is, no matter how much sin there is, God's grace is greater than that sin. God's grace is enough to cover it, to forgive it, and to cleanse us from it.

Yes, a very powerful thought, indeed.

But it's also a thought that can easily lend itself to misapplication.

In fact, that was the very text Rasputin used to justify his sinful ways. His logic went like this, *Well, if my sin causes God's grace to abound, and if God's grace is a good thing, then I might as well sin all that I want.* Thus, the Mad Monk, pulling these verses out of context, used it to give himself license to engage in his degenerate lifestyle.

And as the history of the last century has shown, that misapplication had some very dire consequences.

But the apostle Paul's point in Romans was anything but what Rasputin took from it. In fact, in Romans 3, Paul condemned this type of perverted logic. He wrote,

> Why not say (as we are being slanderously reported and as some claim that we say), "Let us do evil that good may come"? Their condemnation is just (Romans 3:8, NASB).

Thus, it seems that even in Paul's day there were those who misinterpreted the good news of salvation by faith to mean that they could do anything they wanted to.

Paul condemned that kind of thinking and announced that those who held to it were guilty—that it is possible to presume too much upon the grace of God, to use it as a justification for continued rebellion against God, and to receive condemnation for it.

When Paul wrote that "where sin abounded, grace abounded much more," he was again expressing the truth that we focused on earlier. And that is, no matter how great the sin problem is, the solution—Jesus Christ's death on the cross—is enough to solve it. What the first Adam messed up, Jesus, the Second Adam, more than fixed.

Paul is telling us that God's grace is sufficient to cover all the wrongs that we have ever committed. The point is, no matter how bad our pasts have been and no matter how guilty we might be, there is hope for all of us. And that hope is based on what Christ has done through His death on the cross, and the salvation it brings to us as sinners.

Thus, we must not fall into Satan's trap in which our sins held before us, we feel too unworthy to be saved. When that happens, we have to tell ourselves that Christ came to die for sinners and that Christ came to die for us *precisely because* we are unworthy. And yet, despite that unworthiness, we are reckoned righteous through the righteousness of Jesus, which is given to us by faith. Or as Paul said at the beginning of the chapter: "Therefore, having been *justified by faith,* we have peace with God through our Lord Jesus Christ" (Romans 5:1, NKJV; emphasis added).

Yes, that peace comes because of what Christ has done on our behalf. We don't look to ourselves for that peace. Trust me, you won't find it there. It is found only by looking to Jesus and to what we have been promised in Him.

When we claim those promises for ourselves, when we experience that peace for ourselves, we'll know the reality of these words for ourselves:

I am persuaded, that neither death, nor life, nor angels, nor principalities, nor powers, nor things present, nor things to come, nor height, nor depth, nor any other creature, shall be able to separate us from the love of God, which is in Christ Jesus our Lord (Romans 8:38, 39, KJV).

But when we have this peace in our hearts, this peace with God, what effect does it have on our lives here on earth? Does it change anything, or does it simply make us feel better about ourselves? We'll take up that question in the next chapter.

The Wages of Sin
Romans 6

Evelyn Waugh was a British writer in the first half of the twentieth century. Many of his books were comedies—commentaries and satires on the haughtiness and pretensions of the English aristocracy. In his early years, he considered himself an agnostic, but by the age of thirty he had become a devoted Christian. And though Waugh's books were considered very funny, as a person, he was anything but. His personality was somber and morose, and he wasn't regarded as a particularly nice person to be around. Once, after he berated a young man over some trifle, someone had asked him how, as a professing Christian, he could treat someone that way.

"Without supernatural aid," he said, "I would hardly be a human being."[1]

This idea of "supernatural aid" leads us right to where we are in our study of the book of Romans. For five chapters now, we've been looking at Paul's inspired commentary on the human condition, which could be described in one word: *bad!* The human condition is bad. All we have to do is go online and read the day's headlines and we can see just how bad it really is. Someone once quipped that the Christian doctrine of human sinfulness is one doctrine that you don't need faith to accept.

I agree.

And yet, Paul's other main point, directly related to his commentary on human sinfulness, is that through the righteousness of Jesus, any one of us—regardless of just how bad we are—can be justified before God. That means you can be considered righteous, holy, even innocent in God's eyes.

The Wages of Sin

And the great news of the gospel is that any one of us can have this promise, and it comes not by works of the law but by faith in Jesus. In other words, you can't earn salvation. It is a gift, a gift of God's grace offered to every sinner who claims it by faith.

Paul ended Romans 5 with these wonderful words:

But where sin abounded, grace abounded much more, so that as sin reigned in death, even so grace might reign through righteousness to eternal life through Jesus Christ our Lord (verses 20, 21, NKJV).

That is, no matter how badly you have sinned, no matter how much sin has "abounded" in your life, you can have the promise of "eternal life through Jesus Christ our Lord."

This wonderful news leads right into the first verse of Romans 6. After giving us this promise about grace abounding "much more" than even our sin does, what does Paul immediately write?

"What shall we say then? Shall we continue in sin that grace may abound? Certainly not! How shall we who died to sin live any longer in it?" (Romans 6:1, 2, NKJV).

Knowing human sinfulness, knowing how the human mind works, and knowing how this truth has already been distorted, Paul instantly deals with the great error that goes like this, *Well, if I am saved by grace, not by works, then works don't matter, so I can go on sinning.*

(I can't help but wonder in passing whether there wasn't a little bit of this attitude in Waugh's response. Is it possible that he needed to let a bit more of the grace of Jesus filter into, and out of, his life? I can't judge.)

Paul hits that error right here, fast and hard and with no compromise. In fact, pretty much the rest of chapter 6, *the whole chapter itself,* is Paul giving us the other part of the good news, which refutes that erroneous conclusion about what salvation by grace means. And what he says is that we now have a new life in Jesus, a life in which we are no longer slaves to sin, slaves to the habits and actions that so often bring misery into our existence. Indeed, Paul uses some very powerful images to illustrate what happens to a person who has been saved by grace.

He writes,

> Or do you not know that all of us who have been baptized into Christ Jesus have been baptized into His death? Therefore we have been buried with Him through baptism into death, so that as Christ was raised from the dead through the glory of the Father, so we too might walk in newness of life (verses 3, 4, NASB).

Paul says that for the believer in Jesus, the one who has been justified, two things happen. First, he or she is baptized into Christ's death. The old self dies and is buried with Christ in baptism. The old sinful person has been put to death. But that death is followed by a resurrection, just as Jesus was resurrected. And this is a resurrection to a new life in Christ—a life in which you are no longer a slave to sin.

He goes on like this for a number of verses until he writes, "Even so consider yourselves to be dead to sin, but alive to God in Christ Jesus" (verse 11, NASB).

Again, the same pair of thoughts and the same contrasts: sin and death in contrast to life and Jesus. This is the message of Romans 6. You have been justified by faith, saved by the righteousness of Jesus. You have a whole new standing before God in heaven. Your name is, in fact, written in heaven.

And so, how can you go on as before?

The Wages of Sin

You can't.

You don't.

You died to your old self and are now alive in Jesus.

Now, one of the most misused texts in all Scripture comes amid Paul's discourse here. Continuing this theme, that of no longer being a slave to sin, he writes, "For sin shall not have dominion over you: for ye are not under the law, but under grace" (verse 14, KJV). God alone knows how many people have used this verse to argue that under the New Testament covenant of grace God's law is no longer binding.

But that's not what Paul is saying. Instead, he is saying that you are no longer under the *condemnation* of the law but under grace. The law can no longer condemn you because you are covered in the righteousness of Jesus, whose perfect law-keeping is credited to you by faith.

As if anticipating how that verse would be misused, Paul writes in the next verse: "What then? shall we sin, because we are not under the law, but under grace? God forbid" (verse 15, KJV).

Because the Bible teaches that "sin is the transgression of the law" (1 John 3:4, KJV), let me rephrase that text: *What then, shall we break God's law because we are not under the condemnation of the law, but under grace?* And Paul's answer is, *God forbid.*

The gist of Romans 6 is that we don't have to be slaves to sin, slaves to lives lived in continual violation of God's law, because we have been given new lives in Jesus.

It hardly makes sense for Paul to be talking about sin as he does in this chapter if, somehow, the very thing that defines sin—the law—is done away with. Indeed, in Romans 3, he dealt with this same question: "Do we then make void the law through faith? God forbid: yea, we establish the law" (verse 31, KJV).

Grace and the faith needed to receive it don't do away with God's law. What's the need of grace if there is no law to condemn us? *The law is precisely what shows us our need of grace.* That's probably what Paul meant when he said that through faith in God, by claiming His grace, "we establish the law." We show that it's still to be kept.

Romans 6 is clear; as believers in Jesus, we are no longer slaves to sin. That's good news. We can be freed from the habits and passions and desires that so easily dominate our existence. Isn't that a wonderful promise? I mean, who doesn't want to be free from these things?

Now, let's get this straight, too—this wonderful truth doesn't mean that once you accept Jesus, suddenly all temptations go away and you will never transgress again. No doubt that's a truth that Evelyn Waugh himself could testify to.

If *only* it were that easy. If *only* the moment we accepted Jesus our sins all simply vanished out of our lives. If *only* the moment we gave ourselves to Jesus we suddenly overcame all sins, all character defects, and all the flaws in our personalities. But it just doesn't happen that way. Trust me—I'm all the living proof you'd ever need that that's not what happens. We are going to look at this whole question in more detail in the next chapter, Romans 7.

Rather, it means that you are no longer *dominated* by these things. You will still struggle with them, and you will still fall at times. The key is to die to self daily and live in the power freely offered you in Christ. As often as you do that, you will no longer be a slave to sin.

Paul ends Romans 6 with this verse: "For the wages of sin is death; but the gift of God is eternal life through Jesus Christ our Lord" (verse 23, KJV).

Look at the contrast. The *wages* of sin, what you earn with it, is death. In contrast, Paul talks about the gift, "the gift of God"—which you don't earn. It's a gift, which means that it's given to you. And that gift is "eternal life through Jesus Christ our Lord."

Romans 6 is a powerful chapter, filled with the promises of power, the power that will enable us to be free from the *dominion* of sin in our lives. But we have to claim that power, and we have to make personal daily choices to die to self so that the Lord can work in us and do what is promised us in Romans 6 and all through the Bible. We have to cling to the Lord and cling to what Evelyn Waugh called this "supernatural aid." When we do that, by faith claiming these promises of victory over self and new lives in Christ, we can be free from the dominion of the flesh and of sin and of so much of the pain that sin brings.

In light of such promises, I again with Paul say,

For I am persuaded, that neither death, nor life, nor angels, nor principalities, nor powers, nor things present, nor things to come, nor height, nor depth, nor any other creature, shall be able to separate us from the love of God, which is in Christ Jesus our Lord (Romans 8:38, 39, KJV).

It's interesting, though, that the next chapter in Romans describes a Christian's struggle. Chapter 6 presents us with the hope that we will be victorious as we die to self and live for Christ. Chapter 7 gets down into the nitty-gritty of how this works.

---

1. Clifton Fadiman and André Bernard, eds., *Bartlett's Book of Anecdotes,* rev. ed. (New York: Little, Brown and Company, 2000), 563.

Wretched Man That I Am
Romans 7

Tadeusz Borowski was a Gentile Pole who was held as a political prisoner at Auschwitz. Conditions were terrible for him, of course, but as a political prisoner he didn't have it as bad as many others did. In fact, he survived and later wrote about his experiences. One of his works, a book of short stories, was titled *This Way for the Gas, Ladies and Gentlemen.*

One of the most-remembered scenes in his writings concerned a soccer match at Auschwitz. A group of prisoners, Gentiles, were playing soccer when, behind them, a trainload of deportees arrived. The soccer players stopped, looked at the people being unloaded onto a platform, and then turned around and went back to their game. After a few minutes, Tadeusz, playing goalie, looked back and saw the platform. It was empty.

In one of the most haunting lines to come out of the Holocaust, he wrote, " 'Between two throw-ins in a soccer game, right behind my back, three thousand people had been put to death.' "[1]

The coldness, the indifference, the sheer lack of emotion in the line has been commented on for decades. Thousands of people standing there, about to be killed, and these men go back to their soccer game!

My point here is not to say that they were evil or even complicit in what was happening. They were, after all, prisoners.

Instead, what this story reveals is how—being immersed, as they were, in death on such a vast scale—they were no longer horrified by it. They were, in a very sick way, used to it, that's all.

Who hasn't had a similar experience with something bad? I

mean, the first few times you see it or hear it, you are appalled, frightened, and disgusted. But then, after a while, it stops causing such a negative reaction. Until, finally, it no longer bothers you at all. You simply get used to what used to appall you.

It's human nature. We adapt. Sometimes that's good. I mean, you wouldn't be much of a surgeon if you never got used to the sight of blood, would you?

Oftentimes, though, we get used to bad things. Things that once bothered us we become accustomed to. It takes time, but we get hardened. And this is especially true of sin. We get *hardened* to it.

In our study of Romans, we have seen that though we are sinners, though all of us are guilty before God, the wonderful news of the gospel is that forgiveness is there for us—no matter our pasts. And it's there because of Jesus and His death on the cross. With that death, He paid the penalty for our sins so that we never have to ourselves.

And we have seen also that though we can have forgiveness, this forgiveness doesn't come from obeying the law. It comes from faith in Jesus, whose perfect obedience is credited to us. I love the way author Ellen White states it. Talking about Jesus, she said,

> If you give yourself to Him, and accept Him as your Saviour, then, sinful as your life may have been, for His sake you are accounted righteous. Christ's character stands in place of your character, and you are accepted before God just as if you had not sinned.[2]

That's very good news, isn't it? Paul knows it too. But then he has to confront a question, *If we aren't saved by the law, why is there need to keep it?*

And here's where we pick up Romans 7, where Paul is again dealing with the fact that the law and obedience to the law aren't what make us right with God. In the first six verses, he talks about how we have been freed from the law, in the sense that we have been spared the penalty that the law would bring on us because of our violation of it. "But now we are delivered from the law" (Romans 7:6), that is, we are no longer under the threat of condemnation from the law. We have been delivered from it.

Then, as if anticipating what this good news would bring, what does Paul write?

> What shall we say then? Is the Law sin? May it never be! On the contrary, I would not have come to know sin except through the Law; for I would not have known about coveting if the Law had not said, "YOU SHALL NOT COVET" (verse 7, NASB).

This is a theme that Paul dealt with earlier in Romans and now comes back to. And the question is, *Just because the law doesn't save you, is it somehow nullified or done away with? Does this mean we don't have to keep it anymore?* And his answer here, as in other places, is an emphatic No! Paul then states very clearly that the law shows us what sin is. The law points out sin. "I would not have come to know sin," he wrote, "except through the Law."

In discussing the fact that the law points out sin, Paul then talks about the struggles that he himself has in doing what he knows is right, in seeking not to sin. He starts this lament about how much he wants to do what is right, but he finds himself struggling with the carnal nature that tempts him to do wrong.

Tempted to do wrong when you know what is right? Can anyone relate?

Wretched Man That I Am

He writes,

> For the good that I want, I do not do, but I practice the
> very evil that I do not want. But if I am doing the very
> thing I do not want, I am no longer the one doing it, but
> sin which dwells in me (verses 19, 20, NASB).

I speak for myself here, but I find it *very* comforting to know
that even someone like Paul, the *apostle* Paul, had a struggle with
sin.

All of which leads to a crucial point. Why should we as
Christians fight against sin anyway, fight against the sinful cravings and desires of our fallen nature as we see Paul doing here?

I mean, can't we be forgiven? Isn't that the whole point of the
gospel? Didn't Jesus, when asked by Peter if he should forgive a
brother who sinned against him seven times, respond, "I do not
say to you, up to seven times, but up to seventy times seven"
(Matthew 18:22, NKJV)? Seventy times seven? Isn't that Jesus'
way of saying that no matter how often he sins against you, you
have to forgive him? And doesn't God do the same for us?

The answer is Yes *if* we seek for that forgiveness and *if* we
claim it for ourselves. But here's the big problem, and it goes
back to what I said earlier. *We get hardened in sin.* Let me repeat.
We get hardened in sin. The more we do it, the less evil it appears
to us. Paul knows that we can be forgiven our sins. But he also
knows that the more we sin, the less sinful it appears to us, the
less appalled we are going to be by it, and thus, the less likely we
are to come back to the Lord and seek the forgiveness that we
need.

Sin doesn't drive God away from us; no, it drives us away
from God and from a saving relationship with Him.

Have you ever wondered why Satan tempts Christians into

sin? Satan knows the Cross. Satan was *at* the Cross. Satan knows the Bible too; he knows that there is complete pardon for anyone who comes to Jesus, and who confesses and repents and claims the righteousness that Jesus offers us all.

Why, then, does he want Christians to sin? Because the more we sin, the less sinful it will appear to us, and thus we are less likely to see our own need of Christ. We think, *Oh, it's not so bad, not really,* and we go on our merry way, totally deceived about our relationship with God and our true standing before Him.

Perhaps, in all of the Bible, the clearest example of this principle is Judas Iscariot. Why did Satan enter Judas, as Luke says, as opposed to any of the other disciples, who were nothing to write home about? The answer, I believe, is that Judas was hardened in his heart, hardened in the sin that he harbored there. And because of that sin, he refused to surrender and claim the forgiveness and pardon and victory that Jesus would have freely offered him.

Jesus didn't reject Judas; no, *Judas rejected Jesus*—and Judas stands as a symbol of anyone who, having a saving relationship with Jesus, allows sin to nullify that relationship.

What, then, is the answer? Or as Paul, at the end of this discourse about his struggle with sin, expressed it: "O wretched man that I am! who shall deliver me from the body of this death?" (Romans 7:24, KJV).

Wretched man that I am? Paul, the saintly, fervent, zealous author of so much of the New Testament, cries out, *Wretched man that I am?*

And who shall deliver this wretched man?

The wretched man answers his own question: "I thank God through Jesus Christ our Lord" (verse 25, KJV). Paul then goes right back to Jesus, to the promises found in Jesus and in His righteousness, which include the promises of victory over sin.

Yes, we are, like Paul, in a battle with the flesh, with sin, and with self. But if we live in daily surrender to Jesus, if we live in daily submission to Him, we will have victory over the sin that seeks to dominate us. And yet, at the same time, if we fall and if we start to get discouraged by our sinful state, we must always lean upon His righteousness, clinging to it with all our hearts and souls and might. If we do that, we will never turn away from Jesus, and Jesus will certainly never turn away from us.

Which is why, we can be persuaded, as was Paul, that

> neither death, nor life, nor angels, nor principalities, nor powers, nor things present, nor things to come, nor height, nor depth, nor any other creature, shall be able to separate us from the love of God, which is in Christ Jesus our Lord (Romans 8:38, 39, KJV).

Yes, there are still struggles in the Christian life, even after we come to realize that God loves us amid it all. And chapter 8 gives us a strategy for dealing with those struggles. It helps us realize that even when things get the best of us, we need not feel condemned. That's the message we'll consider next.

---

1. Tadeusz Borowski, *This Way for the Gas, Ladies and Gentlemen,* ed. and trans. Barbara Vedder (New York: Penguin Books, 1976), 84, quoted in Ruth Franklin, "The Writing Dead," review of *Postal Indiscretions: The Correspondence of Tadeusz Borowski,* trans. Alicia Nitecki, ed. Tadeusz Drewnowski, *The New Republic,* September 24, 2007, 47.

2. Ellen G. White, *Steps to Christ* (Washington, D.C.: Review and Herald® Publishing Association, 1956), 62.

No Condemnation
Romans 8

When Elvis Presley died in 1977, his long-time manager, Colonel Tom Parker, is reported to have said, "This changes nothing."[1]

This changes nothing?

I suppose what the Colonel meant was that he and Presley's other close associates—often called the Memphis Mafia—didn't need a living Elvis to enable them to continue milking the cash cow of Elvis's music.

So, maybe for the Colonel and the Memphis Mafia Elvis's death didn't change much. For Elvis, though?

Yeah, it changed things. (The testimony of those who continued to report Elvis sightings for years afterwards notwithstanding!)

In Romans, the apostle Paul talks about death. But not the kind of death that leads to a funeral. He talks about a death to self, a death to sin, a death to the flesh. And though this death doesn't apparently change things as radically as a physical death does, it does change things.

This is the death that comes when we accept Jesus into our lives and commit ourselves totally and unreservedly to Him. This is a death that comes to self and to sin when we claim for ourselves Jesus' righteousness and perfection in place of our own sinfulness and imperfection.

As we have seen, according to Paul in the book of Romans, all of humanity, Jew and Gentile alike—we are all evil, we have all been corrupted, and we are all under the condemnation of sin. There are no exceptions. Rich or poor, male or female, young or old, fat or skinny, white or black or anything in between—it makes no difference. We are guilty.

But Jesus Christ came into this world, lived a life of perfect holiness and perfect righteousness. And the great news of the gospel, of what is called justification by faith, is that we can claim by faith the perfect righteousness of Jesus as our own. And when we do, it becomes credited to us as if it were our own holiness and our own righteousness. We become justified in Him; that is, we are made right with God, not because of anything that we have done but only because of what Jesus has done, which is credited to us. And, as I have been saying all along and can't stress enough, it becomes credited to us—by faith and not by the works of the law.

Then, as a result of this new standing before God, our lives are changed. We have died to self, died to sin, and died to the old ways, which we once lived. We now have new lives in Jesus.

Yet, as Paul showed in Romans 7, we still have struggles with sin. We still have battles to fight. We still don't always live the way we should. We are still sinners in need of God's grace.

And this leads right to the beginning of Romans 8, the last chapter we will cover in this study. Paul begins this chapter with some of the most famous words in the New Testament: "There is therefore now no condemnation to them which are in Christ Jesus, who walk not after the flesh, but after the Spirit" (Romans 8:1).

Let me repeat, there is, therefore, now "*no* condemnation."

No condemnation. Zilch. Nada. None. Though you are a sinner, though you have done wrong, though *you are still* a sinner, and though you *still might do* wrong—God's Word tell us that there is "no condemnation."

That's because your sins have been forgiven for Christ's sake. His perfect life covers your imperfect one. You can stand before

God in full assurance that you are accepted by Him, not because of your own works, but because of Jesus' works, which are credited to you by faith.

Talk about wonderful news!

But I would be remiss if I were to stop here with just the wonderful promise that "there is therefore now no condemnation." Let me read again the whole verse, so that we can get the whole picture, because the wonderful news doesn't stop there. "There is therefore now no condemnation to them *which are in Christ Jesus, who walk not after the flesh, but after the Spirit*" (emphasis added).

No condemnation to those who are *in Christ Jesus*. And how do we know that we are in Christ Jesus? It's because we walk not after the flesh but after the Spirit.

What we see here, in this one verse, is a very concise summary of what it means to be a Christian, of what it means to be born again, and of what it means to have a new life in Jesus Christ.

Paul emphasizes two main points about our life in Christ. First, as we saw, there's the "no condemnation" part. We are justified in the sight of God because we have the righteousness of Jesus Himself, a perfect righteousness, credited to us. We stand perfect in the eyes of God. And it's totally by God's grace.

At the same time, however, we have new lives in Jesus, lives in which we walk not after the flesh but after the Spirit. This means that we are no longer slaves to the carnal nature and slaves to the cravings of our sinful flesh. Instead we walk in the newness of life that we have in Jesus. He lives in us and transforms us.

Though Paul has touched on this latter part throughout the beginning chapters of Romans, his main emphasis was on the former—on the part about being justified by faith alone. He spent a great deal of time making that point, the most wonderful point, I might add, in the entire Bible. And that's because it answers the age-old question that Job had asked, "But how can a man be righteous before God?" (Job 9:2, NKJV). He can be righteous before God through faith in Jesus.

And now that Paul has established that point, here in Romans 8 he really hammers home the kind of life someone justified by faith will live.

Listen to what he says,

> For those who are according to the flesh set their minds on the things of the flesh, but those who are according to the Spirit, the things of the Spirit. For the mind set on the flesh is death, but the mind set on the Spirit is life and peace, because the mind set on the flesh is hostile toward God; for it does not subject itself to the law of God, for it is not even able to do so, and those who are in the flesh cannot please God (Romans 8:5–8, NASB).

Paul contrasts those have experienced the reality of grace in their lives with those who haven't. Those who haven't don't obey God's law; they can't because they are slaves of the flesh, slaves to their carnal nature.

Yet, the good news is that through Jesus we become new people. His Spirit dwells within us. This happens only after we die to self, a death that does, indeed, change almost everything about us.

Paul continues,

> If Christ is in you, though the body is dead because of sin, yet the spirit is alive because of righteousness. But if the Spirit of Him who raised Jesus from the dead dwells

in you, He who raised Christ Jesus from the dead will also give life to your mortal bodies through His Spirit who dwells in you (verses 10, 11, NASB).

Look at the contrasts here—death and life, flesh and spirit, sin and righteousness. What he is saying here, as he had said in Romans 6, is that Lord, who raised Jesus from the dead, has the power to give us life. He has the power to keep us from doing the things that lead to eternal death. And that is because God's Spirit dwells in us.

What we see here in Romans 8 is a full expression of what it means to be a Christian. We are justified by what Christ has done for us; as a direct result of what He had done *for* us, He begins a work *in* us. And this is a work that changes the way we live because we are now dead to sin but alive unto the Spirit that takes up residence in our hearts.

So then, brethren, we are under obligation, not to the flesh, to live according to the flesh—for if you are living according to the flesh, you must die; but if by the Spirit you are putting to death the deeds of the body, you will live (verse 12, NASB).

I don't know how Paul could put it in any plainer terms. If you live according to the flesh, that is, if you let your sinful nature dominate, *you must die.*

But, if you live by the Spirit and live in submission to God, then He will give you the power to put to death the clamors of the fallen nature. The great news is that through Jesus we don't have to be slaves to our sinful habits. We can have victory over the things that so often bring misery to ourselves and to our loved ones.

No Condemnation

In short, we face either life or death. And only we, by our choices, can determine which fate will be ours. And what a tragedy to choose anything other than Jesus and the promises He has for us—promises of pardon, promises of life, and promises of victory over sin.

We must look to the Cross, to what Christ suffered in order that these promises could be made real in our lives. And, by looking at the Cross and realizing who that was and what He was doing *for us*—I, along with Paul, can surely exclaim,

> For I am persuaded, that neither death, nor life, nor angels, nor principalities, nor powers, nor things present, nor things to come, nor height, nor depth, nor any other creature, shall be able to separate us from the love of God, which is in Christ Jesus our Lord (verses 38, 39, KJV).

---

1. Alanna Nash, *The Colonel: The Extraordinary Story of Colonel Tom Parker and Elvis Presley* (New York: Simon and Schuster, 2003), 312.

If you have been blessed by this booklet and would like to help us keep spreading the good news of Jesus Christ through preaching, teaching, and writing, please send your donations to

Voice of Prophecy
P.O. Box 53055
Los Angeles, CA 93055

www.vop.com